The C

Christine Economos

This is a coral reef.
It is made up of tiny animals called corals.

Many other sea animals
live in the coral reef, too.

A blue tang fish lives here. The baby blue tang fish is yellow.

As it grows, it changes color.
It turns blue.

Orange and white clown fish live here.
They stay near an animal
with green tentacles.
Can you see the green tentacles?

The clown fish hides
in the tentacles
to keep safe.

A green lettuce slug lives here.
How did this animal get its name?

It looks like lettuce, but it doesn't taste like it!

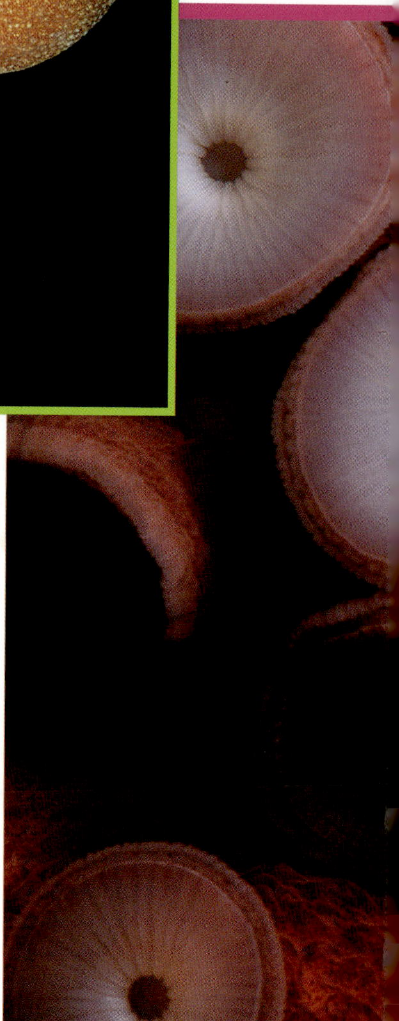

An octopus lives here.
Can you see the many
circles on its eight
long arms?

These circles help the octopus taste and feel.

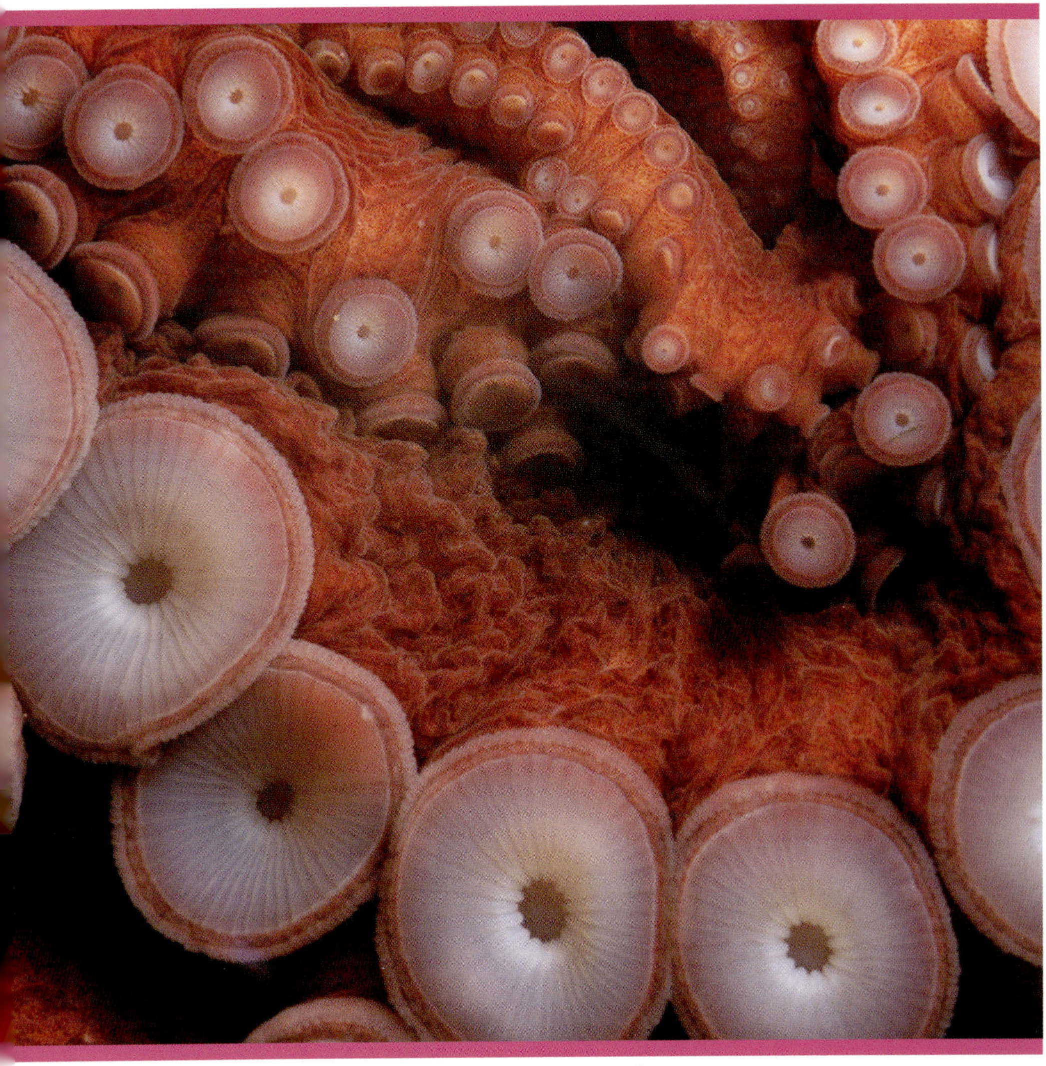

A big blue clam lives here.
Can you see the black dots?

The black dots are the clam's eyes.
Its many eyes help the clam
see danger.

A puffer fish lives here.
What happens when it
is in danger?

It puffs itself up.
Then it looks scary.

Index